# Some Ideas for Beautifying Your House

# Table of Contents

# Introduction

Has the thought of selling your home in the near future crossed your mind? If so, it is a good idea to review how your home might appear to a prospective buyer.

It is no secret that a well maintained, clean and appealing home has a far better chance of selling, at a higher price and more quickly than a home that could use some work and attention.

Keep in mind that first impressions always create lasting impressions. Nothing could be further than the truth when it comes to real estate.

Of course, this does not mean you need to embark on a major renovation project in order to sell your home. There would be no guarantees you would be able to recoup the costs of such a large and expensive project.

Instead, it is better to take a more conservative approach and look at the possible cosmetic improvements which can be made to create an overall improvement. Such improvements might include refinishing, painting, cleaning, etc. These projects do not require much in the way of capital; however, they can make a tremendous improvement to the overall look of your house.

Before you take on any projects; however, it is important to remember that you are fixing up your home for the purpose of selling it. Avoid personalizing the improvements you make as this can limit your market. A limited market means you will usually endure a slower sale and possibly a lower sales price.

Your goal should be to make the home as clean, attractive, well maintained and presentable as possible. One the home is sold the new owners can handle their own customizations.

In this guide, we will cover all the most important aspects of your property and discuss the ways in which you can get the most from your home's sale without the need to spend a large amount of time or money.

One of the most important projects you can undertake when trying to sell your home is improving its "curb appeal."

Therefore, it is a good idea to begin sprucing up your home on the exterior and then work your way to the inside of the home. Start by walking around the home and the lawn to gain an idea of what needs to be improved. The items you notice can then be used as a checklist to be sure you are on the right track.

# Outside your Home

Remember that the outside of your home is the first thing potential buyers will notice about it. If the outside is appealing, prospective buyers will want to view the interior as well. This is why it is important to begin working on the outside first.

**Tidy Up**

Begin by working your way around the property, picking up all the waste and refuse you find. After you have finished picking up and throwing way all of the trash, make another tour of the property and do away with any clutter that might be present. Clutter may include:

- Yard care tools
- Kids' toys
- Bicycles
- Tools

Simply removing all of the clutter and refuse can make a huge difference to the exterior appearance of your home.

**Trim the Shrubbery**

Shrubbery and other greenery around your home that has taken on an unkempt look can be seen as a sign of neglect by prospective buyers.

Make and effort to keep the shrubs and bushes neatly trimmed and shape to provide an overall impression that the entire property has been well-maintained and cared for. For an additional touch, work to keep the shrubbery in line with all other greenery as well as outdoor decorations present on your property. This will create more of an appealing appearance from the street level and create more interest as well.

If your shrubbery has grown so large that it makes approaching your property difficult, it could well be time to consider taking the shrubs out altogether. Remember that shrubbery that is too large will make your home appear smaller and can also create a safety hazard.

A couple of hours should be all it will take to get the job done. This is an inexpensive task that you can handle yourself; however, if you simply do not have the time or the ability or even the inclination to handle the job consider hiring a professional. The job will cost between $35 and $45 per hour; however, it will be well worth this small investment in the end when your home is sold.

**Plant Flowers**
Flowers, particularly bright flowers can go a long way towards livening up the exterior of your home in an easy and inexpensive manner. The flowers you plan need not be exotic or expensive. Even cheap, low maintenance flowers such as the following will work well:

- Marigolds
- Petunias
- Zinnias
- Sweet asylum
- Bachelor's buttons

Your local garden center will be able to help you in choosing the best selections for your location. Keep in mind; however, that annuals tend to be less expensive than perennials and they will work just fine.

Try to mix a few bright colors such as yellow and pink to provide a happy appearance to the home. Plant your flowers in containers on porches, in flower beds and under windows to create varying levels of warmth and depth.

**Landscaping: Mow the Lawn**
A well manicured lawn is a sign of a property that has been well cared for. When you are trying to sell your home the landscaping of the front as well as the back should look its very best. Landscaping will add a huge contribution to the overall resale value of your property. In fact, homes with excellent landscaping tend to sell for 5% higher than homes with inferior landscaping. Homes with poor landscaping can even sell for as much as 10% less. Obviously, this is a huge difference in the overall selling price of your home.

So, how much time and money should you dedicate to the landscaping of your property while trying to sell? Keep in mind that even a minimal amount of time and money will aid in selling your home as well as getting an increase in the sales price. Each effort you make will be worth it.

That said; however, you should not overdo it. Landscaping is not meant to be a selling feature, it is only something will help in the appearance of your home.

Your lawn should be mowed in a manner so that it is even and short. Take the time to keep it well weeded and use a weed eater for the edges to provide a superior finished touch.

If you notice any bald or bare spots in your lawn, take the extra step to purchase a bad of seed and fill the spots in. This can be particularly important if you have pets that dig. After you fill in the dead spots, be sure to water the areas, especially after your pets go outside. Watering those areas will dilute the urine and prevent it from burning the grass.

Be sure Porches and Railings are in Good Repair

Porch railings tend to become wobbly and may appear worm over time after exposure to the elements. This can be a safety hazard as well as appearing unattractive. Review your railings to determine whether they need repair. In some cases, railings may simply need a bit of tightening in the bolts. An adjustable wrench can be used to tighten them quite easily.

If the railings have been screwed into the brick of your home the sheath may have become worn down or broken. In that case, you will need to replace the sheath. This is not costly or time consuming. It can be performed in under half an hour and you can purchase the materials needed at your local hardware store. Simply remove the screws and the sheaths. The railing will come down, so place it aside for the moment. Put the new sheath in place and screw the railing back on.

**Maintain the Shutters**

Shutters can add a charming touch to any home. When in good shape they add a comforting, warm touch to any finish. If they are not well maintained; however, they can quickly make a home appear neglected. The good news is that it does not require a lot of time or skill to repair shutters. With most shutters, a quick sanding and one to two coats of exterior house paint will make your shutters look good as new.

Ideally, it is best to remove the shutters before you begin sanding and painting them. First, clean them of any dirt and then give them a light sanding. Wipe them down again to remove dust particles from the sanding. Now, you are ready to paint.

You may opt to spray paint or brush paint. Either choice will provide a nice result. Be sure to allow them to dry completely before reattaching them to the home.

**Touch-up Painting**

Many homes are made of brick with wooden trim. Generally, wooden trim is located on porches and on the ends of the home. As time passes, the wood trim can become worn and the paint may become cracked and dull.

A bit of touch-up paint can give your home a fresh new look. Depending on the amount of trim you have, it should not take more than three hours to complete the task.

In some cases, you may need to sand areas before you can paint them. Sanding will help the new paint to cure better than applying it directly to old paint-especially if there was a cracked surface. A palm sander will work well for this project.

**Be Sure your House Numbers are Visible**

This can seem like a little matter; however, it can make a big difference when selling your home. Potential buyers must be able to find your home in order to consider buying it.

If your house numbers were carved into the exterior surface, take the time to make sure they can still be seen from the street. If you find it is difficult to read them, paint the numbers using a crisp clean color so they are readily visible.

If the numbers have been mounted on the house, be sure they are in good condition and match your home. Are they still stylish? If not, replacing them is an easy and inexpensive matter that will make a huge difference in providing your home with a modern, updated look.

**Make the Front Entrance Beautiful**

The front entrance to the home, including the porch, nearby windows and front door is tremendously important. Remember that this is where prospective buyers will pause first and be given the opportunity to gain a very up close impression of your home. Therefore, you want to make sure it has tremendous appeal.

The door should be sharp in appearance. It necessary, give it a fresh coat of paint. Take the time to be certain that the hardware is polished or freshly painted. Other ideas on ways you can beautify the entrance include:

- Painting or replacing the mailbox
- Installing bright porch lights
- Providing a new welcome mat

Be sure as well that the doorbell, if you have one, is working.

**Exterior Cleaning**
Next, take a look at the overall building and ask yourself the following questions:

- Are the windows clean?
- Is the siding clean?
- Are the gutters clean?
- Are the corners free from spider webs and vines?
- Is the walkway clean? Does it have a defined edge?

Checking all of these items can easily be done in a little time and make a tremendous difference in selling your home.

# Inside your Home

After the outside of your home has been improved it is time to move to the inside of the home. There are several projects you can tackle on the inside, without spending a lot of money or time, which will make a huge difference.

There are two primary areas in your home which should be focused on; the bathrooms and the kitchen. The following tips will help to guide you through the process of sprucing up the inside of your home to make sure you realize its maximum potential when you sell it.

## Decorating

Today, the world of real estate is becoming amazingly sophisticated. The idea of staging a home for sale has, in fact, revolutionized the world of real estate. It does not take a large amount of money; however, in order to produce an effective result. It simply involves improving the current surroundings.

Begin by looking through your home through the eyes of a prospective buyer. Pretend you have never seen your home before.

## Create Space

Clearing out excess furniture is a great way to start. Pieces of furniture that are too large for the room in which they are placed or that crowd a room should be removed. Place them in storage for your upcoming move, give them away or sell them.

Work on clearing out excess accessories as well including collections. When it comes to opening up a home there is truly nothing more effective than removing clutter. This will provide your home with a more spacious appearance quite easily.

## Surface Space

Next on the list is to go through the house and clear all of the horizontal surfaces in the kitchen and bathrooms. Do not leave any knick-knacks, magazines or other items. Pack them or get rid of them.

## The Importance of Smell

Your home should always smell nice. Unfortunately, over time we tend to become accustomed to smells in our home. To help combat this problem have a non-pet owning, non-smoking friend come over to give your home the sniff test. When it comes time to sell the house; however, there should be no noticeable odors. Work on getting rid of smells such as:

- Cigarette smoke
- Pet odors
- Stale food smells

Smells can make a tremendous impact on prospective buyers when they first enter a home. Avoid adding artificial scents; however, such as using a spray air freshener as more and more people are exhibiting allergies. The best way to rid your home of odors is not to cover them up. Instead, remove them by:

- Scrubbing the entire house
- Replacing old carpet
- Smoking outdoors
- Cleaning the air vents

## Buyers are just as Human as You

When selling your home it is important that buyers are just as reluctant as most homeowners to take on large projects. Generally, they want to move into the house they have bought and be happy with it as it is.

If your property is in need of work, it really is better to go ahead and tackle the projects before prospective buyers begin seeing the house. You always want buyers to see all the house has to offer not envision all that needs to be done to it.

Projects might include:

- Removing old carpeting
- Replacing old, outdated wallpaper
- Repainting cracked or peeling paint
- Replacing cracked, broken or missing tiles

Keep in mind that with each change that a prospective buyer sees they may have to make to a property, the chances of selling the property for the desired price dwindles. Take the time to handle these projects to assuage any possible such concerns.

**Baby Safe**

If families with babies or young children are part of your potential market it is imperative that you ask yourself whether you would feel comfortable putting your own child on the floor to crawl around.

To make sure your home can pass any concerns young families might have, first be sure it is absolutely clean:

- Do the floors look clean enough to eat off?
- Do the carpets look and smell fresh?
- Are the walls free of grime?

**Cigarette Smoke**

The smell of cigarette smoke is the last impact you want a prospective buyer to have of your home. This goes much beyond the smell; however, which can be quite offensive to many buyers. The look of ashtrays, even clean ones, as well as smoke stains on cupboards and walls can also be unappealing.

It is important to take sufficient action so that your home will appear as though it has never been smoked in. Ideally, there should be no evidence that would alert buyers of your habit.

Take the time to store ashtrays out of sight, clean the walls, ceilings and any other places that could retain vestiges of cigarette smoke. Cover or replace any carpets, upholsteries or fabrics that have burn holes.

If you feel you must smoke, do so outside but make sure you do not leave any stray cigarette butts behind.

**Timeless Appeal**

There can be a huge difference between a classic home and an old home in the world of real estate. Just as there is a comparable difference between vintage clothing versus old clothing, there is a huge difference when it comes to homes.

Two 40-year old homes are not necessarily the same. If your home still have 40 year old paint and wallpaper, 40 year old appliances and 40 year old appliances, sadly; you have an 'old' home.

If; however, you have maintained your home with a good established look, kept everything fresh and up to date; you have a 'classic' home, which is very appealing.

**Light Things Up**

Prospective buyers look for two things in a home: light and space.

So, while it is quite all right to have a home that is somewhat on the darker side, if the entire room is dark there could be a big problem.

When prospective buyers view your home, make sure you open blinds and drape, turn on all of the lights and even add lights to rooms which might be darker.

You can also actually suggest sunlight in rooms by adding flowers and other touches. This can be helpful during the winter months or simply on days when Mother Nature is not that helpful in providing natural light.

**The Importance of a Professional Home Inspection**

Generally, most homebuyers will obtain a professional home inspection; however, if you make an effort to do this ahead of time you gain the ability to take care of any repairs before you home goes on the market.

Depending on the type of home you have and your area, you can typically expect to pay between $200 and $400 for a home inspection; however, it can be well worth the cost. Ask your real estate agent and he or she should be able to recommend several local inspectors.

**The Classic Appeal of Plain White**

Bright, bold colors have become very popular today; however, they can be a problem when you are selling your home. This is because you and your buyer may not share the same tastes in colors.

The good news is that paint is a relatively inexpensive and easy way to provide your home with a fresh new look. When selling your home, it is important to stick with neutral colors.

White, cream and beige can may seem somewhat boring; however, they can make it much easier to sell your home. White will also reflect the most light of any other color and as a result can also make rooms appear larger; a huge selling point.

## Looking at your Carpet

If you have carpet, it is a good idea to have it shampooed in order to remove any smells or stains that might exist. If shampooing it does not do the trick, you may need to get rid of altogether.

If your only alternative is to get rid of the carpet, it may be wise to think of using wood or laminates instead of simply replacing the carpet. Both wood and laminates are much better selling features. They make your home appear more spacious and buyers in today's market tend to prefer them. In addition, they are also easier to keep clean.

## Do Not Make a Statement with your Decorating

While your current decorating style may suit you fine, this can be another matter when it comes to prospective buyers. If your home has a decorating style that is intended to make a statement, it can be a good idea to tone it down some while your home is on the market. Examples might include:

- Controversial art
- Taxidermy mounted on the wall
- Risqué sculptures

## Wallpaper: Either it Sticks or Remove It

If your home has peeling wallpaper it should be immediately removed and replaced with a fresh coat of paint.

This is particularly important in bathrooms and kids' rooms. In the bathroom, remove the wallpaper and paint the walls a pleasing neutral shade.

For kids rooms, choose colors that are as neutral as possible as well.

This will allow buyers to see the home for itself, not your decorating style. It also enables them to imagine how their own belongings will look in the home.


**Clean out the Closets**
Buyers are always looking for a good amount of space to store their own things; so it is a good idea to straighten and clean out your closets.

A good way to approach this is to take everything out of your closets and only replace half of it. The remainder should be donated, sold or stored in another location, out of the home.
A partially empty closet looks far roomier than one that is crammed. Storage and space sell, so this is an important project to tackle.

This same guideline should also be applied to other storage areas, including kitchen cabinets. When it comes time to move; however, at least you will have had the opportunity to sort through your stuff and get rid of many things that you will no longer need to transport when you move.

**Fresh Flowers**
Fresh flowers can give your home a bright, clean and healthy look without spending a lot of money. One way to handle this to add a professional arrangement of flowers to your home while it is on the market. If you would rather spend the money on something else; however, you can always choose a few less expensive flowers and arrange them yourself.

Ideas for affordable, fresh cut flowers include:

- Daisies
- Carnations
- Irises
- Asters
- Freesia

You might consider having the colors of the flowers match the season as well as the room.

For example, in the spring, there is a good opportunity to use pinks and purples while summer is great for reds and bright yellows. In the fall, consider pale yellows and oranges. When winter rolls around, opt for anything bright and happy.

**Open up the Windows**
If the weather is mild enough outside, opening up the windows can be a great way to bring in fresh air and get rid of any smells that you might not have even noticed.

Do be careful about the temperatures when opening the windows; however. If you make the rooms in your home too cool or too hot, prospective buyers may feel uncomfortable and will not become as attached to the home. Even worse, they may feel as though the home would be difficult to keep warm or cool.

**The Importance of Cleanliness**
The importance of cleanliness cannot be stressed enough. When people look to buy a home, they are generally more observant and even picky than they would normally be. You never want to lose a sale simply because of something small.

So, it is a good idea to go over your home with not only a fine tooth comb but a white glove as well to be sure it is really spic and span. Pay close attention to areas such as:

- Cobwebs
- Dust
- Trash
- Grime

**Make your House Stand Out**

In today's market, most home buyers will see numerous homes. It is not at all uncommon for buyers to see at least a dozen homes, so it is important to make sure that your home is the one that will stand out in their minds.

There are good ways; however, to make your home stand out and then there are bad ways. At all costs, you must avoid the bad ways of making your home stand out. Focus on the good ways instead.

Consider this for a moment. If you saw five houses this week and another five next week, how much do you really think you would remember about each house? Chances are you would only remember one special little detail.

Taking the time to add those special little details that will make your home more memorable will increase your chances of selling. Aim for adding something that is different and positive to set your home apart from all of the others prospective buyers will view.

**Be Realistic**

As much as you want to maximize the selling potential of your home it is important to be realistic and remember that you do not want to go so far that you have not only wasted your time but possible overwhelmed prospective buyers.

If you go too far in your efforts, the house will begin to feel artificial. This should be avoided. You want your home to feel warm and inviting. It should feel like a home.

Buyers should feel as though they could move in right away not as if they are in a museum where the sign says "Look, do not touch."

## Different Rooms of the Home

There should be three primary goals in each of your rooms:

1. Remove any personal items such as family photos, posters, trophies, items from the fridge doors, etc.

2. Clear out high traffic areas by removing excess furnishing and belongings.

3. Highlight the primary features in each room such as French doors, fireplaces, etc.

# The Kitchen

The kitchen and the bathrooms tend to be the most scrutinized rooms of the house. Therefore, these rooms should be you first priority. This does not mean undertaking a complete or expensive remodeling. Real estate experts concur that remodeling your kitchen is not always cost effective when you plan to sell.

There are some great small things you can do in terms of minor improvements and generally sprucing things up; however, that will provide a great impact on both the speed of sale and the sales price of your home.

### The Kitchen Sink

There are several little tasks that you can handle in and around the kitchen sink that will make quite a bit of difference but which are easy and inexpensive.

For example, you should make sure there are no leaks. Take the time now to be absolutely sure there are no leaks and you will not have any surprises later on when prospective buyers are visiting.

It is also a good idea to remove any stains from the sink itself as well as surrounding areas. Make sure the sink and sink hardware shines. This can be as effective as replacing it.

**Kitchen Appliances**

Even if you do not plan to leave your kitchen appliances behind, you should be sure they are well cleaned and shine like new. This includes providing a thorough cleaning of the:

- Refrigerator

- Oven

- Dishwasher

- Toaster

- Microwave

- Coffee maker

This is particularly true for any appliance you will be leaving behind; however, giving everything a thorough cleaning will provide an overall impression of a well-maintained, sanitary and friendly kitchen.

Appliances, which are dirty, make prospective buyers feel as though the rest of house is dirty as well. Even if everything is immaculate except for one small thing; that one little bit of grime could be enough to change the entire impression the buyer has of the home.

**Kitchen Cupboards and Cabinets**

Provided your cupboards and cabinets are in good condition, there is no need to

replace them and spend a lot of money.

To give them a bit of a facelift, you can simply make sure they are clean and well kept.

This can be done by:

- Replacing out of date, old hardware

- Applying fresh, white shelf paper

- Wiping down cupboards to eliminate smudge or fingerprints

- Applying a fresh coat of paint on cupboards that cannot be wiped clean

**Kitchen Surfaces**

There should be no clutter in your kitchen whatsoever. If there is anything in your

kitchen that is not absolutely necessary it should be removed.

Remove any floor obstruction, clean out the cabinets and clear off the table and

countertop.

This will open up your kitchen and provide a much cleaner and even more spacious

appearance.

In today's market, buyers want large kitchens. They desire room for their own

belongings as well as room in which to move around. If you cannot demonstrate that

your kitchen has that, they will look for a home that can.

**Your Kitchen and Paint**

A simple coat of fresh pain can rejuvenate your entire kitchen. With a fresh coat of paint applied to the ceiling, walls and cabinetry, you can literally take years off the appearance of your kitchen and make it look much cleaner.

Focus on using neutral colors that will make your kitchen look cleaner and larger.

**The Center Island**

If you want your kitchen to have a custom look and you have a sufficient amount of room in which to work, consider connecting two or three stock base cabinets and overlaying them with a new countertop to create an island. Allow room on one side for bar stools.

**Introduce Flair with Molding**

If your cabinets are somewhat on the plain side, consider using molding to give them a more luxurious look. Picture or regular panel molding can redefine doors and drawers that are flat.

You might also consider adding elaborate crown molding where your cabinets meet the ceiling to create an appearance that is elegant and classic.

**Make a Splash with a Backsplash**

Inexpensive glass mosaics, natural slate, porcelain tile or even a faux paint finish can be used to create a backsplash that is both unique and custom.

**Light Things Up**

Adding lighting to your kitchen will increase the appeal as well as the appearance of size and overall brightness. Lights can be added almost anywhere in a kitchen. Possible ideas include:

- Above cabinets
- Under cabinets
- From the walls
- From the ceiling

**Dress up the Windows**

There are many different window treatments that can be added to add to the appeal of your kitchen.

Venetian blinds, Roman shades and wood blinds are all great ways to add style while keeping out the glare of the sun.

If your kitchen has more of a country style, consider adding lace or some other type of fabric curtains to provide a warm and pleasant appearance.

# The Bathroom

Any effort you can make in the bathroom will add value to your home. Before you immediately jump on a project; however, it is a good idea to take a good look at potential problems and issues that might exist.

Remember that bathrooms can be somewhat tricky. As much as you may want to maximize the appeal of the bathroom, and even though this room is a major selling point, you also do not want to invest a lot of money in a project that simply will not pay off when you sell. Instead, it is important to focus on simple cosmetic improvements rather than overhauls and renovations.

**Bathroom Fixtures**

Take a long hard look at your bathroom fixtures before you immediately go to work on them. Ask yourself these questions:

- Are the fixtures cracked, damaged or leaky?
- Are they stained or dirty?
- Are the fixtures outdated?

If the answer to any of these questions was yes, then it can be a good idea to consider taking one of the following courses of action.

- Replace or repair seals or fixtures for those that are cracked, damaged or leaky

- Avoid replacing fixtures with expensive options. Instead, select fixtures that are attractive enough to enhance the bathroom but are not obviously lavish

- Use a quality bathroom cleaner to remove any stains, grim or buildup.


**Bathroom Moisture**

Moisture is certainly an inherent part of any bathroom and it can be a real hassle when it comes to creating a grimy appearance as well as encouraging the growth of mildew.


Take a look around your bathroom and ask yourself the following questions:

- Are there any visible water stains on any surfaces?

- Are any of the finishes damage by moisture?

- Is there any mold growth anywhere?

- Is any of the paint blistering or peeling?

- Is any of the grout or caulking cracked, peeling or chipped?

- Are there any surfaces that are buckled, swollen or rotten?


If you answered yes to any of these questions, then review the following courses of action to deal with these issues.


- Find out if any of the moisture is coming from plumbing leaks, building leaks or high levels of humidity. Fix the cause if at all possible.

- Repair or replace parts of the bathroom that are damage or deteriorating

- Remove any visible growth of mold using a quality cleaning product that is designed for that specific purpose

- When possible, keep the window open to increase ventilation and release excess humidity

- Repair or replace grout and caulking

**Plumbing and Electrical in the Bathroom**

To make certain the electricity and the plumbing are up to date in the bathroom, ask the following questions:

- Do the pipes make a banging noise?

- Is the water pressure unsatisfactory?

- Do the drains flow slowly?

- Are there any unusual smells or noises in the drains?

- Is the lighting sufficient?

- Is the electric wiring adequate and safe?

If you find you are faced with any of the issues listed above, you may want to choose one of the following methods to improve the situation:

- Install water pipes with a larger diameter. This will allow for greater flow.

- Be sure your drainage system is vented sufficiently and that proper traps are installed

- Unclog drains so they will drain more freely

- Have an electrician inspect the wiring. Upgrade as necessary for safety reasons

- Update the lighting so it is adequate

**Keeping it Clean and Neat**

When a prospective buyer views your bathroom it should always be spic and span clean

as well as neat. This includes the toilet, sink, walls, mats, floor, counter and tub.

Be sure the counter space is clear so that it looks as large as possible. De-personalize

the space so that buyers can imagine the space for their own items.

# The Front Entrance

Besides the bathrooms and kitchen, the front entry can be the most influential in the home when it comes to creating lasting first impressions.

This is typically the first area of the home a prospective buyer will see so it can be helpful to add a fresh coat of paint to the door and/or walls.

Be sure the floors are extremely clean as well to give an appearance that is fresh and sanitary.

Also make sure there is plenty of light in the front entry. Keep all of the lights on and open up any existing blinds to maximize light. The brighter the entry appears, the more appealing the home will be.

# Bedrooms

Bedrooms are also closely observed. Therefore, they should always be presentable.

The beds should be made and look as though they are in a hotel. The entire space should be clutter free as well as free from personal items. This will create a space that looks larger as well as allow buyers to imagine their own belongings there. Be sure the closets are tidy and organized.

# Living Room and Dining Room

Both of these areas should be clear with only enough furniture in them to create a welcoming feel. Remove any extra furniture.

In addition, remove any photographs, knick-knacks and other personal items. All areas should be dust free.

# Final Touches

Now, that we have worked our way through all of the main rooms in the house and you have an idea of what should be expected overall, we will review some final tips to provide your home with that extra special touch which will set you and your home on a path towards a successful sale.

### Windows

Take the time to clean your windows until they sparkle. Remove any paint splatters using a razor blade. A mixture of ammonia and water will work wonders for creating shiny windows

### Gleaming Floors

Your floors must be spotless and absolutely gleaming. Wash your floors until you can see your reflection and then add a new mat at the front door.

### Provide a Place for Umbrellas and Coats

Too many umbrellas and coats in the entry can give a cluttered look. Remove extra items here, keeping only one per family member.

**Keep Things Simple**

When it comes to the walls, too many pictures can make a space feel crowded and

small. Either hang one large picture or a grouping of smaller pictures.

33

**Install Higher Wattage Bulbs**

Higher wattage bulbs will provide additional illumination, resulting in rooms appearing

larger.


By using these tips you can ready your home for a fast and profitable sale!